SPECIAL BONUS
YOUR FREE GIFT

60 PAGES OF PRINTABLE **FUN**

PLAYFUL PENCILS
WHERE LITTLE MINDS FLOURISH

MY FIRST

ABC & 123

60 PAGES OF PRINTABLE FUN

FIND US ON AMAZON

Scan me

More from playful pencils

Preschool Kids Activity Book

Cut and Craft
Alphabet Art Adventure
FUN LETTERS
SCISSOR & STICKING SKILLS

Dear Dentist
I LOST MY TOOTH
MY TOOTH LOSS JOURNAL

PLAYFUL PENCILS
WHERE LITTLE MINDS FLOURISH
MY FIRST & 123
PAGES OF PRINTABLE FUN
FIND US ON AMAZON

PLAYFUL PENCILS
WHERE LITTLE MINDS FLOURISH

This Book belongs to:

....

Draw your smiley face

PLAYFUL PENCILS
WHERE LITTLE MINDS FLOURISH

PLAYFUL PENCILS
WHERE LITTLE MINDS FLOURISH

PLAYFUL PENCILS
WHERE LITTLE MINDS FLOURISH

ABC

Playful Pencils
WHERE LITTLE MINDS FLOURISH

Playful Pencils
WHERE LITTLE MINDS FLOURISH

Playful Pencils
WHERE LITTLE MINDS FLOURISH

Playful Pencils
WHERE LITTLE MINDS FLOURISH

PLAYFUL PENCILS
WHERE LITTLE MINDS FLOURISH

Playful Pencils
WHERE LITTLE MINDS FLOURISH

PLAYFUL PENCILS
WHERE LITTLE MINDS FLOURISH

Playful Pencils
WHERE LITTLE MINDS FLOURISH

PLAYFUL PENCILS
WHERE LITTLE MINDS FLOURISH

PLAYFUL PENCILS
WHERE LITTLE MINDS FLOURISH

PLAYFUL PENCILS
WHERE LITTLE MINDS FLOURISH

PLAYFUL PENCILS
WHERE LITTLE MINDS FLOURISH

PLAYFUL PENCILS
WHERE LITTLE MINDS FLOURISH

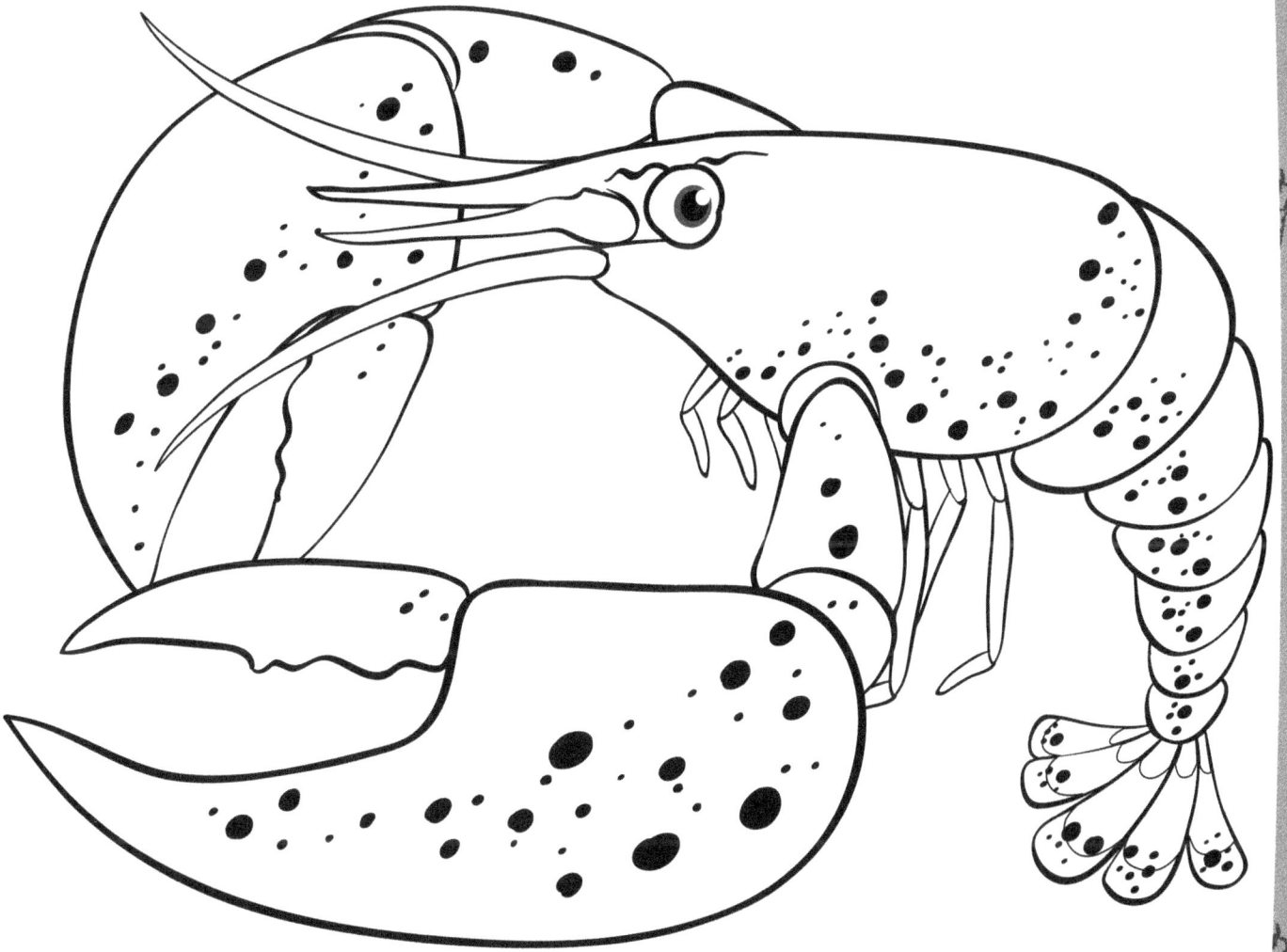

PLAYFUL PENCILS
WHERE LITTLE MINDS FLOURISH

Playful Pencils
WHERE LITTLE MINDS FLOURISH

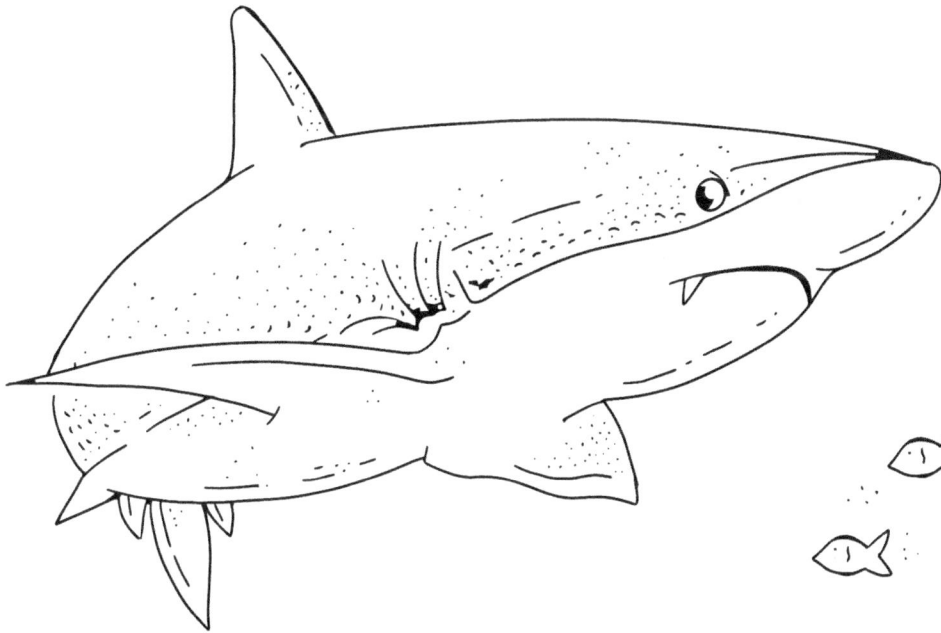

SPECIAL BONUS
YOUR FREE GIFT

60 PAGES OF PRINTABLE **FUN**

Scan me

More from playful pencils

Preschool Kids Activity Book

1

Children Age 3-5

Letters and Numbers

Colors

Fun Activities

Gift Inside

PLAYFUL PENCILS

PLAYFUL PENCILS

Cut and Craft
Alphabet Art Adventure

FUN LETTERS
SCISSOR & STICKING SKILLS

GIFT INSIDE

KIDS WORKBOOK AGE 3-5

ENHANCES FINE MOTOR SKILLS

SPARKS IMAGINATIVE PLAY

PROMOTES HAND EYE COORDINATION

PLAYFUL PENCILS

Playful Pencils
WHERE LITTLE MINDS FLOURISH

I LOST MY TOOTH

MY TOOTH LOSS JOURNAL

PLAYFUL PENCILS
WHERE LITTLE MINDS FLOURISH

MY FIRST
& 123

AGES OF PRINTABLE FUN

FIND US ON AMAZON

Playful Pencils
WHERE LITTLE MINDS FLOURISH

www.ingramcontent.com/pod-product-compliance
Lightning Source LLC
Chambersburg PA
CBHW081226020426
42331CB00012B/3086